ISAAN

FORGOTTEN PROVINCES OF THAILAND

TEXT AND PHOTOGRAPHS BY
BEN DAVIES

This project was made possible through the generous assistance of :

Hotel Sofitel

RAJA ORCHID KHON KAEN

Published in the Bahamas by LUNA Publications Ltd.
Photography & text by Ben Davies

Slide processing : AV Camera, Bangkok - Tel (662) 234 4786
Design, layout & production : Xtra image, Bangkok - Tel (662) 275 2585
Color separation : Express Printing
Printed in Bangkok by Eastern Printing

Publisher : Ben Davies
Publishing Consultant : Thomas Renaut
Picture editor : Roland Neveu
Text Editor : Christopher Burslem

ISBN : 974-89353-4-5

Acknowledgements :
Thanks to the many friends who have contributed in some way to this book, espe-
cially Sakil Nontee in Chiang Khan. Pawat Thanadkha and Akani Tuptimtong in
Bangkok, and of course to Cristina. Also thanks to travelling companions Chris
Gow, Jeff, Elizabeth and Isabelle for their inspiration and good company. Finally
thanks to Roland Neveu and Thomas Renaut for making the book possible.

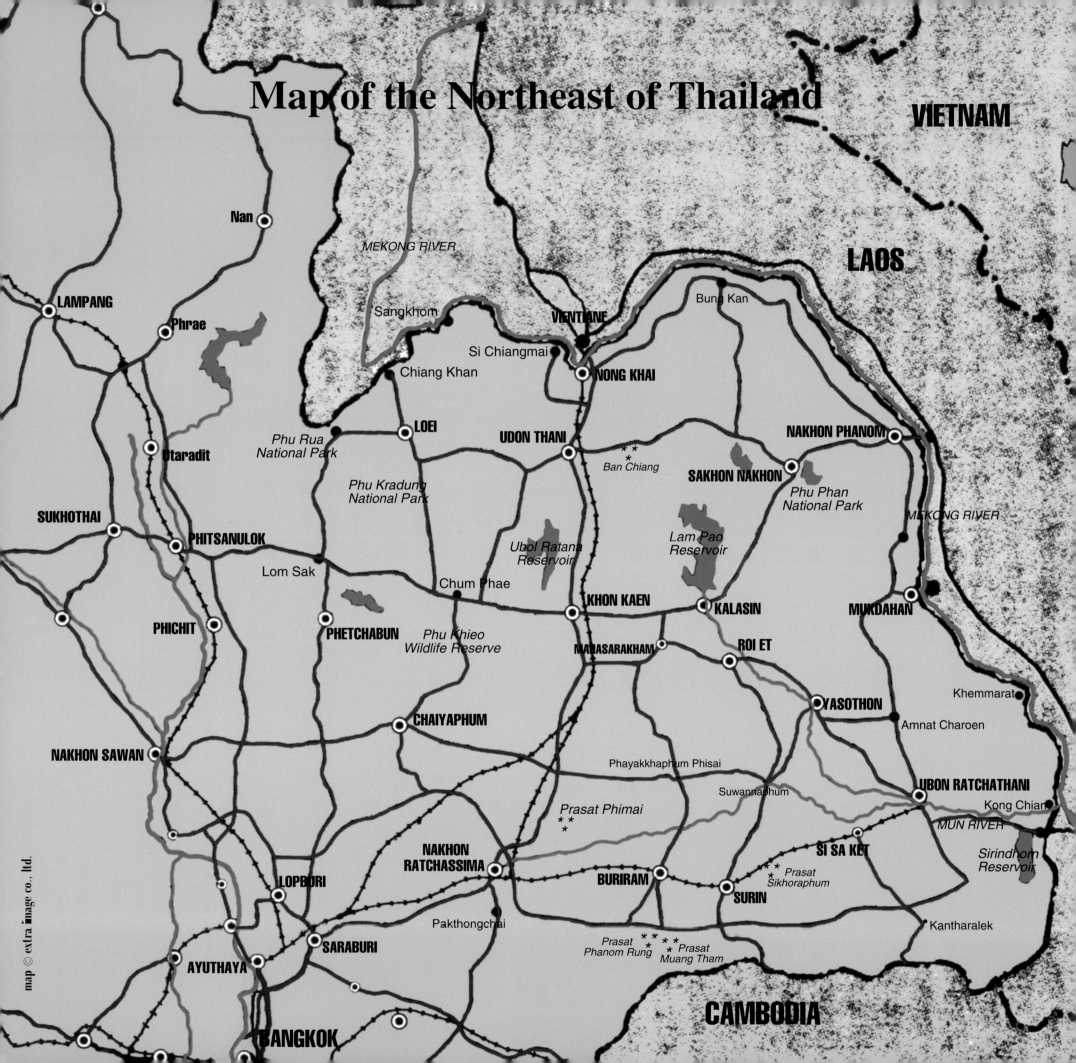

Map of the Northeast of Thailand

VIETNAM

LAOS

MEKONG RIVER

Nan

LAMPANG

Phrae

Sangkhom

Bung Kan

VIENTIANE

Si Chiangmai

NONG KHAI

Chiang Khan

Utaradit

LOEI

UDON THANI

NAKHON PHANOM

Phu Rua National Park

* *
*
Ban Chiang

SAKHON NAKHON

Phu Kradung National Park

Phu Phan National Park

MEKONG RIVER

SUKHOTHAI

PHITSANULOK

Ubol Ratana Reservoir

Lam Pao Reservoir

Lom Sak

Chum Phae

KHON KAEN

KALASIN

MUKDAHAN

PHICHIT

PHETCHABUN

Phu Khieo Wildlife Reserve

MAHASARAKHAM

ROI ET

Khemmarat

YASOTHON

Amnat Charoen

CHAIYAPHUM

NAKHON SAWAN

Phayakkhaphum Phisai

Suwannaphum

UBON RATCHATHANI

Kong Chian

Prasat Phimai
* *
*

MUN RIVER

SI SA KET

Sirindhorn Reservoir

NAKHON RATCHASSIMA

BURIRAM

* *
* *Prasat Sikhoraphum*

LOPBURI

SURIN

Pakthongchai

Prasat Phanom Rung
* *
*   * *
* *Prasat Muang Tham*

Kantharalek

SARABURI

AYUTHAYA

CAMBODIA

BANGKOK

map © extra image co., ltd.

FOREWORD

I will always remember that day in late 1991 when I first left the heat and chaos of Bangkok to drive to Khao Yai and over the invisible boundary into Isaan, the poorest region of Thailand. It was early November and the mornings were filled with mist that covered the endless pastiche of rice fields bounded by a distant horizon. Here and there a few water buffalo bathed by the side of the road, oblivious of the traffic, the heat and the dust.

It took more than three years before I returned with my project up and running. Some things had changed; the new highways, the factories and sprawling urban developments. Along the borders too, commerce was bringing life to districts which had hitherto been tied to the land.

But the feeling of Isaan remained, the stark arid landscape, the fine Khmer temples and the blaze of colourful faces, a fleeting sense of past and present which for me will always make this the most awesome region in the kingdom.

THE FAR PROVINCES

East of Saraburi and the Dongrek Mountain Range, the Friendship Highway climbs steeply, passing giant limestone outcrops and sparsely covered hills before entering a landscape that is harsh, arid and tempered in its beauty. Beyond the town of Pak Chom and the Lam Takhong Reservoir, the mountainous scenery soon gives way to rolling plains, to red sandy soils and to the distant hills of Khao Yai which stretch over vast tracts of land towards the Cambodian border.

Here and there, small villages nestle off the highway, collections of straggling houses and dusty market towns set against a sea of rice and tapioca fields. A few water buffalo languish in the mud, small dots on an endless horizon.

Named after *Ishana*, the Hindu god of death, and occupying the Northeast corner of Thailand, Isaan is the country's least known region, home to a third of its population and to some of its most extreme and desolate terrain. From the barren soils of the Korat Plateau to the lush tablelands of the Phetchabun Mountain Range, the region covers some 170,000 square kilometers, an intricate canvas of contrasting threads that encapsulates some of the most varied scenery on earth.

Squeezed within these borders is a world that bears little in common with neighbouring regions, a land where the feel of Laos and Cambodia is more prevalent than that of Thailand. The ethnic mix in Isaan has given rise to a different flavour. It is a flavour reflected in their food, their spicy *larb moo* and *somtam*, a fiery salad made from grated unripe papaya, fish sauce, garlic and chillis. It is a flavour reflected in their language, a mixture of Lao and Khmer. More than anything, it is a flavour reflected in their unhurried life style, with tricyclists snoozing on their bikes in the shade or rice farmers with their wide-brimmed straw hats picnicking in the paddy fields.

But the people of Isaan also have an unrivalled zest for life. When Isaan people party, they throw all constraint to the wind, dancing down the streets with their bottles of rice whisky and their sound systems blaring out Isaan's own distinctive style of music. Even Buddhism, an inextricable part of Isaan life, is by no means inconsistent with enjoyment as when a young man becomes a monk for a period of his life. On such an occasion, the family will invite relatives from miles around. Then a marquee will be put up and vast amounts of alcohol consumed as the people of Isaan indulge themselves in the ultimate release from their days in the fields.

Rich Traditions

Wherever you travel in Isaan, you will come across tableaus of rural life that come from another age: families bathing in the river or fishing in the rice fields. Indeed, whilst Isaan lacks the beaches and colourful hill tribes of Southern and Northern Thailand, what it offers is far richer and more meaningful: the struggle of human nature over a largely inhospitable environment. Isaan people take pride in their culture, in their dialects and their origins. Above all they relish in the absurdity of their position, rebuffing the attacks of central Thais who regard them as country bumpkins and illiterate farmers.

Beneath the poverty and hardship, however, is a

history that not only belittles that of the remaining country, but which may even place Isaan as one of the cradles of civilization. According to well known Thai archaeologist Pisit Charoenwongsa and a group of anthropologists from the University of Pennsylvania, between 3,000 BC-4,000 BC, this area played host to an advanced culture which may have pre-dated that of neighbouring China and Mesopotamia. In Ban Chiang and in the surrounding villages of Udon Thani Province, magnificent buff pots, bronze tools and burial urns bear witness to a flourishing era of artists and rice farmers. These people not only produced the world's oldest socketed tool, they may also have traded their expertise with empires as far flung as Asia Minor where similar finds are evident. Rich carvings too dot the rock faces of Kong Chiam and along the Mekong River. They include images of hunters, fish and animal traps etched with pigment made from animal blood, vegetable gum and soil.

But like many of the most valuable pots and bronze arti-facts, these early trumpeters of an advanced civilization disap-peared almost without trace, leaving only questions behind them along with thousands of glass beads, necklaces and copper bells.

Successive Migrations

According to historians, an Indianized people known as the Mons migrated from Funan in Cambodia to Isaan sometime between the 5th and the 8th centuries. Little however is known of that period except that these people also dominated a collection of city states around Lopburi.

Of the Khmers who followed, there are few such doubts. These warriors, whose home was Angkor swept down from Cambodia during the 9th and 10th centuries settling in Laos, Northeast Thailand and as far afield as Vietnam and the Malaysian Peninsula. Brave soldiers, these people were also fine architects, leaving as a legacy some of the most exquisite monu-ments known to man. Few other remains in Thailand can compare with the carvings of Prasat Muang Tham, the famous lintels of Prasat Phanom Rung or the thousand year old statues of Prasat Hin Phimai.

It was left for the Europeans to register their impressive-ness more than seven centuries later when they came across ruins spread out over the jungle clearings. "All about lay huge blocks of stones carved deeply with gods and dancing girls, monkeys and warriors," wrote W.T. Blake in 'Thailand Journey' in 1955. "The lintels of the gateways were similarly carved and we were able to appreciate the magnificent workmanship put into this place by the Cambodians in the time of King Nariman I".

Eminent Explorers

Over the years, many of Isaan's temples fell to wrack and ruin, forgotten by the mists of time. When the eminent surveyor James McCarthy arrived in Isaan in January 1884, he had to cut his way through mosquito-infested jungle. On his journey, he crossed malaria swamps as well as districts infested with robbers and evil demons. It took nearly two weeks to travel from Saraburi to Korat accompanied by elephants, oxcarts and 200 soldiers pro-vided by the king.

"For geographical research the frontier region provided a wide and interesting field, for the greater part of it still remained unvisited by Europeans and on the maps the country was a blank," McCarthy wrote in his book 'Surveying and Exploring in Siam'.

French naturalist Henri Mouhot, one of the country's most distinguished explorers and the man credited with the re-discov-ery of Angkor Wat, found Isaan no less memorable. "Korat is a nest of robbers and assassins, the resort of all scum of the Laotian and Siamese races," he wrote in his book 'Travels in Indo-China, Siam, Cambodia and Laos' in 1861. "Bandits and vagrants, escaped from slavery or from prison, gather here like the vultures and wolves which follow armies and caravans". Mouhot found "the inhabitants impertinent and disagreeable" and much prone to "gambling and opium-smoking".

Upheavals

The fierce independence of a people whose origins unite them more to neighbouring Laos and Cambodia than to Thailand also led to massive upheaval. Thai history books prefer to skip over the period from the end of the second world war until the late 1970s. In reality, this period saw Isaan become a hotbed of discontent which spawned not only a communist insurgency movement with strongholds in many of the forests and villages, but even attempts to form a breakaway country.

The situation was aggravated by isolation, with Isaan largely cut off from the remainder of the country by lack of roads and poor communication. Although the first stage of the northern railway line from Bangkok to Korat was completed in December 1900, it took another sixty-five years before the line could be finally extended all the way to Nong Khai. Only in the 1960s, did the threat of communism and widespread concerns for national unity spur efforts by Thailand's government to bring the Northeast Region into the fold.

The start of the Vietnam War signaled the arrival of the modern world in Isaan. During the mid 1960s and early 1970s, the Americans pumped millions of dollars into many of the region's cities, building airports and bases from which to support their war effort in neighbouring Indochina. At one stage Udon Thani housed more than 10,000 American soldiers as B52s took off at night to carpet bomb neutral Cambodia and war-torn Vietnam. To the motley ingredients of GIs were added new roads, new towns, experimental dams, as well as bars, restaurants and anything else to support the war effort and spread a thin veil of prosperity over the region.

Modern Ubon Ratchathani, Korat, Udon Thani and Khon Kaen are the legacies of that war. They were the launching pads for the devastation of Cambodia and Vietnam. But despite the ultimate failure of the US venture in Indochina, the towns have continued to prosper and grow to the point where they ironically serve as gateways between Thailand and its former enemies. Supply centres for tractors, motorbikes, fridges and televisions, they are the harbingers of a new religion that has already transformed much of the country into a consumer paradise.

To wander around these cities, into their shopping centres, their karaoke bars and fast food shops, is to enter a different world. Where once wooden houses leaned precariously along narrow alleyways, the mid 20th century architects have left behind gaudy Chinese shop-fronted houses that are distinctive only in their characterless uniformity. In the busy markets and shopping arcades, local rice farmers arrive to fulfill their dreams, buying plastic buckets and cheap radios, before returning to the familiar world of their villages on crowded buses, *songtheows* and tricycles.

Latest reports put the population of these cities at one or two million, with Korat ranked as the second largest city in Thailand, larger even than the tourist heartland of Chiang Mai and the southern commercial centre of Hat Yai. But whilst the cities now extend their tentacles into the heart of Isaan, they cannot yet claim to have undermined the vitality of a region that continues to flourish.

Diverse Countryside

Outside in the countryside, beyond the factories and the new housing developments, lies the traditional Isaan, a countryside made up of some 20,000 villages, with an estimated three million Lao people and more than half a million Khmers. It is a countryside of rice farmers, of tapioca producers, of salt farms and weavers. More than anything it is a countryside where life remains largely unpolluted by the ever approaching world called progress.

In this forgotten region, the land meanders from one extreme to the other, beautiful and desiccated by turn. From the busy town of Korat, face of the new Isaan, it is a giant leap back in time to the sleepy banks of the Mekong River where the glutinous brown waters flow down through the Northeast, leaving behind a vein of fertility. Along the border, sudden twists and turns in the road offer tantalizing views over to Laos with its gentle backdrop of thatched fishing villages, its lush forests and undulating hills beyond. Occasionally too you may see streams and rapids crisscrossing the rugged slopes, strange fissures etched upon the tropical landscape.

Further to the west beyond the towns of Udon Thani and Nong Khai, lie the mountains of Loei Province and the national parks of Phu Kradung, Phu Luang and Phu Rua. Amidst this natural splendour, where the landscape of Africa mixes with the pine trees of Europe, wild buffalo and monkeys can still be seen along with emerald doves, silver pheasants and woodpeckers. High up on these slopes shaded by bamboo and tropical evergreen, you will also find rhododendrons, azaleas and wild orchids flourishing in the temperate climate.

Any journey to Isaan, however, would be incomplete without a stay in Buriram, in Chaiyaphum and in Surin wherein lies the heart of Isaan with its rice farmers and cattle herders, its silk weavers, and its markets piled high with barbecued chicken and sticky rice. This is the place to wander and savour rural life, untouched by the winds of change and to feel for a moment the simple power of times gone by.

Changing Seasons

In Isaan the seasons colour the landscape with a harsh loveliness. During the winter months, early morning mist hangs over the valleys and plains, a thin veil of down that soon dissipates beneath the midday sun. Along the Mekong River, the cries of fishermen mingle with the gentle sounds of rushing water, gift from the monsoonal rains. At dawn too, the paddies come alive with villagers harvesting the rice that will provide their families with a source of food in the long months ahead.

At these times, moments last like the taste of some sweet fruit to be savoured and remembered. But in the fierce heat of May, the fields begin to crack and even the rivers turn to streams pierced by jagged boulders. As temperatures soar to as high as 40C, activities in the villages almost cease, save for the morning parade of monks from the temple and the day's work at the little village school.

Paradoxically it is at the height of the dry season that the trees blossom with bursts of red, white frangipani and yellow cassia set amidst the dead trees and twisted deciduous branches. It is also in the midst of the heat that the mood of despair gives way to some of Isaan's biggest celebrations: to *Songkran* and to the rocket festival, celebrations which bring new hope to the people of Isaan.

Literary Flavour

It is little wonder that those moods have inspired some of Thailand's greatest literary writers, men like Kampoon Boontawee and Pira Sudham who tell of the precarious existence of peasants in the underprivileged Northeast and of the callous and more sophisticated way of life embodied in the West. 'Monsoon Country', published in 1988, was inspired by Sudham's own upbringing in a remote village in the district of Napo, and in its loving evocation of the simple lifestyle enjoyed by the people of Isaan, it is one of the most poignant records of those changing times. The story tells of Prem Surin, the son of poor rice farming parents who is catapulted from his simple roots into the upper levels of Western and Thai society. Yet in his new life in London, amidst the splendour of a Hydepark flat and the trappings of wealthy expatriates, it tells of his longing for the monsoon plains of his childhood and of the pain of evolution and progress.

It is a theme that is common, not only in Sudham's later novels and essays, but in works by other writers from Isaan. In Kampoon Boontawee's 'Child of the Northeast', an award winning novel that was subsequently turned into a film, we are transported back to the 1930s and to a time of famine when vast areas of the countryside were laid to waste. It is a tale of a loving family pitted against the harsh world of Isaan. But what shines through the poverty and suffering is the quiet endurance and courage of the parents known simply as Koon's father and Koon's mother as well as the indestructible and earthy sense of humour of a people who for generations have made this land their home.

"Our lives are subject to the mercy of nature: floods, drought, disease and scarcity" writes Pira Sudham in the introduction to People of Esarn in 1987. "With endurance, we accept our fate as something we cannot go against".

Inner Conflicts

For many Isaan people that conflict remains, torn between the poverty and limited opportunities at home as well as the promise and excitement of the big cities. Every year more than one million seasonal migrants leave the towns and villages of the Northeast for Bangkok, Korat and Thailand's other fast growing industrial centres. And every year, the number increases as Isaan falls further behind the remainder of the country in the league of wealth.

New night clubs, shopping centres and karaoke bars are also springing up in the big provincial capitals of Isaan. Together with the new western style advertisements displayed in market towns and the rags to riches tales that circulate the villages, they guarantee that the days of rural calm will never be quite the same again.

Indeed these days, Isaan has become the reserve of cheap labour, shipped to the building sites, factories and crowded streets of Bangkok. It is the region from where most of the *tuk tuk* drivers and taxi drivers come from and the region from where many of Bangkok's most notorious *go go* bars fill their ranks with young girls. But Isaan is also a state of mind that the people carry around with them. Even in the congested streets of the capital, the thumping bars and corrugated building shacks, there is a relaxed joie de vivre and innocence that comes not from Thailand, but from Isaan mixed inextricably with the flavour of neighbouring Laos and Cambodia.

Quintessential Isaan

The feel of Isaan is also to be found in traditional dances such as the *ram wong*, practiced with respect and austerity in the cities, but acted out with an orgy of exuberance in village festivals. It is to be found in the absurd caricatures of the *likay* where heavily made up boys dress as women in theatrical slap-stick comedies. And it is to be found in the legends of Khun Ying Mo, Isaan's greatest heroine, who fought off the Laotian armies in 1826 during the reign of Rama III and saved Korat from almost inevitable defeat.

In the heartlands too you will discover the traditional Isaan, in the silk-weaving communities, in the Laotian folk tales and the colourful local festivals where giant rockets are fired into the clouds in the belief that this will bring the rains.

But the quintessential Isaan lies far beyond the legends, the Khmer temples and the endless fields beneath ochre skies. It lies in the small market towns and sprawling villages set on the vast plateau. It lies in the simple wooden and concrete houses where generations of families live together in one enclosure. But more than anything, the quintessential Isaan lies in the people themselves, a mixture of dignity, humour, pride and resilience that makes this the most memorable part of Thailand.

Above : Picking flowers, Ban Nok, Surin Province.
Preceding page : Dawn from the hilltop retreat at Wat Phu Tok, Nong Khai Province.

Tropical scenery, Khao Yai National Park, Nakhon Ratchassima Province.

Above : Burning off the rice crop in January, Khon Kaen Province.
Right : Sunset in Phu Kiao Wildlife Reserve, Chaiyaphum Province.

Above : An empty stretch of highway, Ban Phu, Udon Thani Province.
Below : Herding cattle in Prakhon Chai District, Buriram Province.
Left : Early morning at Phu Kiao Wildlife Reserve, Chaiyaphum Province.

Sandstone rock formations, Phu Phra Bat Historical Park, Udon Thani Province.

Above : The great plains of Isaan, Buriram Province.
Following pages : Dawn on the Mekong, Kong Chiam, Ubon Ratchathani Province.

LAND OF THE GODS

At dusk, when the crowds have left the great temples of Isaan, you can feel the silent power of times gone by. For here in this arid countryside, lie some of Thailand's finest surviving monuments, testament to the gods who once held sway.

Probably nowhere else outside of Cambodia can compare with these imposing stone sanctuaries draped in the trappings of another age, with their etchings of the legendary Ramayana and their intricate reliefs. French writer Lunet de Lajonquière in his book 'Le Siam et Les Siamois', described the ornamentation of Prasat Phanom Rung as "among the most perfect of its kind". Others claim that only Angkor Wat and Khao Phra Viharn in Cambodia can excel in terms of their style and scope.

But who were these artists who left behind the temples of Phimai and Phanom Rung, the carvings at Muang Tham and the exquisite lintels at Ban Phluang. And why did they disappear leaving only these ancient shrines of the gods?

According to numerous stone inscriptions, the beginnings of the Khmer empire can be traced to Chenla in Northern Cambodia. During the 9th century, these warriors with their god kings expanded first to Angkor, which was to become their capital, then later to Laos, to Northeast Thailand and as far south as the Malay Peninsula. Under Jayavarman II and a succession of kings, they constructed vast reservoirs and water channels, communication systems and roads. In the mid 10th century, King Rajendravarman II laid the foundations for Prasat Phanom Rung. Less than a century later, work was begun on an adjacent site at Prasat Muang Tham. But it was under the lauded king Jayavarman VII (1181-1219), that the largest number of Khmer-style temples in Isaan were built.

During the 38 years of his reign, this last great ruler of the Khmer empire presided over the construction of Prasat Ta Muen Toch and Prasat Bay Kream as well as Prasat Kamphaeng Noi. Even these monuments however were unable to surpass his ultimate creation: the Bayon Temple in Angkor, acclaimed as one of the finest architectural achievements in history.

Elaborate Carvings

The early Khmer craftsmen had little benefit of cranes or modern day construction techniques. Rocks were transported by cart and artisans worked cutting into the stone using primitive tools. Each of the many thousands of reliefs represents a legendary figure or divine being. For the Khmers believed that the earth was a representation of heaven and that the king was the living embodiment of the universal ruler.

It is little wonder that every corner and every gateway is embellished with elaborate stone carvings. From the central tower, mirroring the peaks of Mount Meru to the moats representing the oceans dividing the heavens from the earth, the details mirror the celestial power of the gods and the relationship between heaven and earth. Even the walls that enclose the temple are used to symbolize the mountains surrounding the heavens.

In Prasat Phimai and Prasat Phanom Rung, probably the greatest of all the Khmer temples in Isaan, the reliefs are of lions, elephants and monkeys, as well as scenes from the Indian epic the Ramayana and episodes from the Hindu creation. Elsewhere beautifully carved five-headed *naga* snakes and lavish sculptures of Vishnu the preserver, Shiva the destroyer and the lion god of Kala bear witness to the Indian inspired ideas which influenced this early civilization.

Such was the religious zeal of the Khmers that by the end of the 12th century, they had built more than 20,000 temples and shrines employing as many as 300,000 priests and temple servants. But the vast resources needed to support this religious empire took their toll. During the reign of Jayavarman VII, the power of the Khmers weakened and from the 13th century onwards they were gradually displaced by the Thais who were to become the dominant power in the region.

Ancient Ruins

When the first Europeans visited the temples of Isaan in the second half of the 19th century, they marveled at the smooth sandstone walls, the elegant gateways with their fluted pillars and the ornamental columns of stucco. "You might here easily imagine yourself among the ruins of Ongcor" wrote the French naturalist Henri Mouhot who visited the temple of Prasat Phanom Wan in 1858. "There is the same style architecture, the same taste displayed, the same immense blocks polished like marble and so beautifully fitted together".

Following the decline of the Khmer empire in the 13th and 14th centuries, many of the religious monuments in Isaan fell to wrack and ruin. In the early 1900s, however restoration work began under Etienne Aymonier and Lunet de Lajonquière. And these days with the support of French archaeologists and the Thai Fine Arts Department, most of the temples in the Northeast have been restored to their former glory.

To see the finest of the temples in Isaan, you must travel north of Korat to Prasat Phimai. Constructed in the middle of the 12th century, shortly before Angkor Wat, this is not just another temple, but a reflection of the Khmer cosmos, with its elegant courtyards and its moats in perfect symmetry around the central *prasat*. Further east in Buriram Province, lie the majestic temples of Phanom Rung and Muang Tham, once connected by road to Angkor, now set amidst rolling hills and rural countryside. To climb the monumental staircase at Phanom Rung, is to take another symbolic journey. For as you pass over the *naga* bridges, you transcend the world of man entering the realm of the gods on the summit of the hill.

Further east in Surin Province on the border with Cambodia, lie the less visited ruins of the 12th century Ta Muen Tam as well as Prasat Ta Muen Toj and Prasat Bay Kream. These small sanctuaries were once Buddhist chapels. Today, although partly tumbled down and over-grown, they still carry a touch of their old worldly magic.

Ban Chiang Era

No less staggering than the great Khmer temples of Isaan are the recent discoveries of ancient pots and other bronze artifacts made in the village of Ban Chiang. Excavations undertaken by the Fine Arts Department and the University of Pennsylvania in the mid 1970s have unearthed more than 18 tons of earthenware pots as well as skulls, tools and jewellery. Initial thermoluminescence techniques date the fired clay pots as early as 4,000 BC with later tests placing them between 2,000 BC and 4,000BC. Even more astounding, these same pots carried the thumb impressed patterns which have been discovered as far afield as Mesopotamia, Iraq and Turkey. But the finds have so far raised more questions than they have answered. Did the people of Ban Chiang emigrate from the Northeast of Thailand taking their potting techniques to other countries, or did some form of trade exist almost simultaneously between Thailand, Asia Minor and even the Americas?

The extraordinary finds in Ban Chiang are not the only ones to have been discovered in Isaan. Other sites have also been unearthed in the provinces of Udon Thani and Khon Kaen, containing glass beads and iron tools. The finds hint at a people that cultivated rice, produced buff coloured clay jars and intricate jewel bracelets. If the recent tests prove correct, they may also have been one of the world's first bronze age civilizations.

Buddhism

As deeply engrained in the history of Isaan as this early civilization is the Buddhist religion, embraced by more than 90% of the people. This religion or philosophy, which was introduced more than 2,600 years ago from Sri Lanka, lays down basic teachings on the path to *nirvana* or enlightenment. According to this path known as the middle way, man must abstain from taking life, he must not steal, he must not lie and he must refrain from using intoxicants and from wrong-doing in sexual matters. For those who become members of the religious order known as the *Sangha*, there are even more rules. Right understanding, right action, right mindfulness, right intention. These are all states of mind that a monk must aspire to. But in their universal appeal and their search for truth, they offer meaning and hope in a world of flux.

In the early mornings, monks still go on their alms rounds offering the people the opportunity to make merit. During the rainy season many of the village men will make candles which will be carried to the temples so that the monks will have light during their three month annual retreat.

Even in the sprawling cities where factories are as much in evidence as temples, the alms round continues, proof at least that religion is not always subservient to economic gain. By making merit, the people believe that they will ensure themselves a better next life on the long road to *nirvana* and to ultimate fulfillment.

Ceremonies

For most Isaan people, the biggest display of faith is reserved for when a layman enters the monkhood. By becoming a novice, even for as little as a month, the man will honour the Buddha and win merit for his parents. Traditionally, it was almost impossible for a man to marry without spending time in a temple.

On the night before he enters the monkhood, the man will celebrate with his friends and family. Then early the following morning, he will have his head shaved before being carried to the temple where he will be presented with robes and an alms bowl. Nobody who witnesses the spectacle can fail to be moved by the sight of the cleanly shaven novice dressed in princely white robes nor by the sheer pride of the family as they carry him through the streets accompanied by village bands and dancing locals. For anything between a week and a lifetime, the novice will remain in the temple. By the time he returns to his home, the young man will have symbolically paid his dues to society and shown his respect for his parents and himself.

Elsewhere Buddhism permeates almost every aspect of life. On religious festivals like *Khao Phansa*, people travel for miles to attend temple fairs or to make merit by offering joss sticks, money and candles. In small shrines reputed to hold a collar bone or tooth of the Lord Buddha, they place flowers and receive holy water, making wishes for the year to come.

At other times of the year, religious ceremonies, spirit exhortations or the worship of past heroes and kings weave unreal patterns into the life of cities and villages of the Northeast. And in their universal reverence for the past and their unadulterated enjoyment of the present, it can almost seem that in Isaan the gods and the spirits still hold sway.

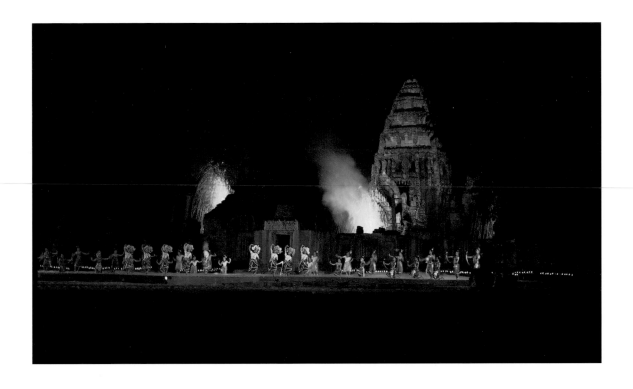

Above : Festival of Light & Sound, Prasat Phimai, Nakhon Ratchassima Province.
Below : Monsoon clouds over the 10th century Prasat Muang Tam, Buriram Province.
Left : 13th century Buddha image, Prasat Phimai, Nakhon Ratchassima Province.

Above : Inner courtyard, Prasat Phimai, Nakhon Ratchassima Province.
Left : Monastic Life, That Phanom, Nakhon Phanom Province.

Stone lions and classical nagas, Prasat Phimai, Nakhon Ratchassima Province.

Above : 12th century Khmer temple, Prasat Sikhoraphum, Surin Province.
Following page : Isaan's most revered temple, That Phanom, Nakhon Phanom Province.

Above : Ancient excavation pit, Ban Chiang, Udon Thani Province.
Preceding page : Statue of Khunying Mo, Korat, Nakhon Ratchassima Province

Dawn over the hill top temple of Prasat Phanom Rung, Buriram Province.

Above & below : Placing gold leaf on the Buddha, That Phanom, Nakhon Phanom Province.
Left : Gift of a lotus flower, Wat Po Chai, Nong Khai Province.

41

Above : A young man becomes a novice, Chaiyaphum Province.
Left : Dressed as a prince in imitation of the Lord Buddha, Chaiyaphum Province.

Offerings to the statue of Khunying Mo, Korat, Nakhon Ratchassima Province.

Above : Makha Puja festival, Chiang Khan district, Loei Province.
Following page : Village portrait, Kalasin Province.

PEOPLE OF ISAAN

It was a summer's morning, three weeks before the start of the rains and the people of Isaan were preparing offerings of rice and flowers for the monks and the spirits. In the sprawling wooden and concrete houses of Kalasin Province, girls as young as five laboured over sticky rice, grinding chillis or cleaning the hearth in preparation for the day ahead.

By the time the sun had risen, most farmers had already left for the fields in rickety old wooden trailers pulled along by mini-tractors. Crowds of school children spotlessly dressed in blue and white uniforms joined the early morning commute, sometimes three on a bicycle or motorbike, or crammed on the roofs of village buses. In the local market a few women dressed in brightly coloured *phaasins* haggle over the price of water melons, onions and red peppers. By mid-morning, the village is deserted but for young children and adults who are too old to work.

Throughout the towns and villages which make up Isaan's 19 provinces, rituals are played out daily, feint echoes of a distant past that continue to colour the present. At dawn, it is still common to see families bathing under a water pipe in the rice fields or catching frogs in the streams to make into curry. In the more remote areas of Kalasin, Roi Et and Si Sa Ket Provinces some of the older people have never travelled to Bangkok. Others recall the days when the only means of transport was an ox and cart or one of the ubiquitous cream-coloured ponies that were used in the jungle lowlands.

Out in the fields, now parched with thirst, a few water buffalo trundle up and down in straight lines, carving out the earth that will soon be flooded by the monsoon rains. Nothing else moves in the stillness of a landscape baked by the searing heat of the sun.

By mid-afternoon, the first children are already returning home from school, carrying satchels and small nets tied on the end of bamboo sticks which they use to catch crickets. In one house, raised on rickety wooden stilts, an old man sits chewing bettlenut, that addictive paste which dyes the teeth a deep red colour and rots the gums. Nearby, in a newer house made from concrete, the whole family sits watching a television purchased a few months earlier with money sent by a faithful son who is working in Bangkok.

Twenty years ago, this scene would have been inconceivable, with oxen carts and the occasional bicycle being the most obvious sign of progress. Since the early 1980s, however, tarmac roads have replaced many of the dirt tracks. Soon cars will be common along with washing machines and telephones. But it will take many more years before the last isolated villages become part of the fast growing tapestry that is now called developed Thailand and the majority of Isaan people finally wake up in the modern world.

Forerunners

Probably the first inhabitants in Isaan settled around 10,000 years ago in the area around the Mekong Valley and the Korat Plateau. These people were not only farmers and hunters, they were also fine potters, painters as well as members of one of the world's first bronze-age civilizations. Over the centuries they were joined by the Khmers who swept across from Cambodia, by the Lao and the Mons, as well as by the Thai Yai and the Thai Noi whose origins are believed to lie in China's Yunnan Province.

From the 18th century onwards, merchants also came from China and settled along the Mekong River at Nong Khai and around Chiang Khan in order to trade in silk and rice with Luang Prabang. Their numbers were swelled in later years by immigrants fleeing the civil wars in neighbouring Cambodia and Laos.

Such diverse ethnic origins set the people of Isaan aside from other regions in Thailand. According to a recent census, there are more than three million Lao people in Isaan, more than in the whole of Laos itself. To these migrants can be added an estimated half a million Khmers.

At night when villagers sit around the fire telling tales of epic battles or mysterious deeds, typically it is not tales of Bangkok or of King Ramkamhaeng, to which they refer. Rather they tell tales of Luang Prabang and Vientiane, cities in Laos, which pre-date much of Thai history and which link them to another age and set of traditions.

Outside their houses too, you are more likely to hear the sounds of Khmer or Lao than the musical rhythms of Thai. Even their food comes not from mainstream Thailand, but from Laos with its spicy *namtoc*, its fiery *somtam* made from shredded papaya, chillis and lemon juice, and its sticky rice, traditionally used to fill the stomach and satisfy the hunger.

Fierce Independence

If history has instilled the people of Isaan with a fierce sense of independence, it has also given them an appearance more akin to their Lao or Khmer neighbours than to the mainstream Thai. Isaan people have darker skins and pug noses, their finely chiselled features more akin to the Mongolian tribes that have intermingled with the native Siamese.

"Even the biggest of the jungle people are most neatly built; they have neither the heaviness of the Chinamen nor the awkwardness of the Ka Che; they seldom run to flesh, and in physical development, with their cleanly chiseled muscles, they are fine specimens of manhood," wrote Herbert Warington Smyth in his remarkable book called 'Five Years in Siam' in 1896.

Warington Smyth, a British national working for the Siamese government, was also much taken by the women folk in the Northeast. "A good many of the women have cut their hair short after the Bangkok fashion, but except for this, all the people retain the best characteristics of the Lao, and are well-built and good-looking as any people we met," he wrote.

A Special Flavour

Isolated from Siam's major towns by the lack of roads, Isaan people until recently had little interaction with the people from other regions. The wild passes and sheer crags of the Korat Plateau gave birth to legends of wandering spirits that would prey on unwary travellers. They also provided fertile hunting grounds for brigands and robbers.

One foreign traveller who visited the far-flung provinces during the 19th century described a region inhabited by dark-skinned peasants much given to "indolence", "opium" and "love-making". Others described a wandering people with little attachment to possessions nor to a traditional homeland. "The people seem to have inherited the roaming propensities of their forefathers who constantly engage in war and either plundering or being plundered seldom had time to become the founders of the city" observed James McCarthy in 1884.

Something of that wild flavour still exists today. It exists in Isaan's raucous markets and the people's exuberant and often bawdy humor. More than anything it exists in their values, a sense of the comedy and temporal nature of life and the cruel twists of fate which leaves them impervious to the rains that bring life to the rice, or the draught that turns their crops to chaff.

In their villages, superstitions flourish as they have for decades. Never have your hair cut on Wednesday. Never move house on a Saturday. Indeed these people can be sufficiently superstitious that the sight of a black dog or a ghekko croaking from behind will be interpreted as a harbinger of bad times. On such occasions, the folk doctor or *maw ya* may be consulted. Then sweet-smelling flowers will be purchased from the market and watches and bank notes intricately shaped from cut-out leaves. These symbolic gifts along with a mouth-watering selection of sweet meats will be used to persuade the *kwan* or spirit of the head to return in order to restore equilibrium to the body and the traditional smile to the face.

Like Koon's father, the hero in Kampoon Boontawee's 'A Child of the Northeast', Isaan people also carry a hardiness that thrives under the most extreme conditions. Traditionally when the villagers were out of food, they would walk for miles to forage for ants or lizards. Yet these people still sang proud songs and told stories of their glorious past. That same acceptance of the vicissitudes of fate enables bar girls from Isaan to put up with working in the big cities in order to send money to their parents or loved ones at home. It also enables husbands to migrate to Bangkok to work on construction sites or as *tuk tuk* drivers in order to support their families.

Simple Life

There is however nothing glamorous about the corruption, the poverty and the injustice which afflicts these same people, driving them away from their homes and their families and into the big cities. Nor is there an easy solution to the disparities of wealth and income which increasingly are opening up a yawning gap between Isaan people and their richer compatriots elsewhere in the country.

Outside of the big cities and sprawling urban centres, extended families live in simple houses raised on wooden and concrete stilts, sharing their meager fare of *larb* and *khao niau*. Afterwards whilst the youngsters sleep on thin mattresses spread out on the floor, the older people will watch the pride of the house, a simple black and white television, or occasionally talk of times of droughts and of wandering spirits seen long before the arrival of roads and motorcars.

In these simple households, where life as a rice farmer was until recently the only option, diffidence and ignorance of the world outside Isaan is widespread. Who cares about a general election when the politicians will no sooner forget their promises. Better to sell votes in exchange for chickens or pigs than to choose a government in a far off city. Often it is the headman himself who will instruct the villagers where to place their votes as few will have heard of any political party. Many of the elders too may be unable to read or to write.

Hardship

But hardship is a word that the people of Isaan have had to live with for centuries. And like the drought and the floods, they have learnt to silently endure. In the new year and especially when the rice fields have been harvested, the people celebrate, drinking the potent local rice spirit known as *Lao khao* and dancing in the streets and around the temple grounds, a release from the rigours of life in the fields.

Even those who have fled the rural villages of Isaan to Bangkok or to the other major cities, will often return on family occasions to celebrate the entry of a family member into the monkhood, to float boats made of banana leafs on the river at *Loi Krathong* or simply to honour their parents and make merit to ensure a better next life.

Drying out the raw silk, Ban Kwai, Chaiyaphum Province.

Above : On the long road back to the village, Yasothon Province.
Following pages : Monks on their early morning alms round, Chiang Khan, Loei Province.

54

Above : Village elder, Mahasarakham Province –
Right, top : Late afternoon portrait, Sakhon Nakhon Province. *bottom* : The local cane weaver, Nong Khai Province.
Preceding pages, left : A young woman road sweeper, Khon Kaen Province– *right* : Tending to the prized fighting cock, Kalasin Province.

56

End of the school day, Si Sa Ket Province.

Harvesting the rice in November, Ban Nok, Surin Province.

An outing in the family car, Si Sa Ket Province.

Above : Children at play, Buriram Province.
Following pages, left : Traditional Bai Si Ceremony, Dan Sai, Loei Province. – *right* : Aged widow, Buriram Province.

MEKONG COUNTRY

Beyond the great city of Ubon Ratchathani, Royal City of Lotus, I caught my first sight of the Mekong, a broad and handsome river that cuts its way through the Isaan countryside bringing life to a region blighted by aridity. From its source high up on the Tibetan Plateau, this giant waterway flows down through Southern China, Burma, Laos, Thailand, Cambodia and Vietnam before emptying out into the South China Sea. But it is here in the upper and lower provinces of the Northeast that the river is at its most varied and accessible.

Known to the Thais as *Mae Nam*, "mother of waters", the Mekong is more than simply a river. Rather it is a life line that holds together the disparate provinces of the Northeast providing not only fertile soil, but a means of communication as well as a source of food and hope. "The mae nam Kong is magnificent," wrote James McCarthy in 1884 summing up the view of many early explorers. "From bank to bank, the river bed measures 1,000 meters".

During the dry season, the river meanders past giant rocks, gentle and deceptively serene as if one could paddle over to the hazy shores of Laos spread out on the far side. At times vast sand banks eat into the river leaving behind channels shaped like octopuses tentacles. But during the rainy season, the river comes alive like some raging animal, its fierce current driving down boats and occasionally flooding the surrounding area.

Ironically it is when the river bursts its banks that the rich sediment from the Mekong brings life to the surrounding fields and villages. During the summer months from April to June the local people catch the giant *pla buk*, monster of the Mekong which can weigh as much as 300 kg and grow larger than a full grown man. Once believed to inhabit underwater caves of gold, these cat fish feed on vegetation and are now acknowledged as the heaviest freshwater fish in the world. At other times of year, the villagers bathe and wash their clothes in the river, using it both as a highway for transport and a source of irrigation.

Mythical Serpent

Legends in Isaan tell that the river is a *naga* or mythical serpent and that every year before the rains arrive somebody must drown in the Mekong as a sacrifice. The local people believe that if the river does not claim a victim, the rains will not come and the crops will die. Along the banks of the Mekong, spirit houses have been erected to ensure peace with "the spirits of water". And in November the villagers float *krathongs* or boats made from banana leaves down the river to give thanks to Mae Nam Kong and to cleanse their soul for the year ahead.

Early reports of the Mekong describe a largely unnavigable waterway that connected the shores of Siam to Laos and the magical town of Luang Prabang. According to a 19th century bulletin of the Paris Geographical Society, it was virtually impossible to go further north than Vientiane. Only the stretch east from Chiang Khan in the far corner of Isaan to the Kemmarat Rapids was navigable. Even then, sailing on the Mekong was fraught with risks. "On April 1 (1896) we started for the South, this time in double boats lashed together with strong crosspieces, on which a light bamboo deck with a rounded cover is placed, forming a very roomy deck-house," wrote Herbert Warington Smyth. "On the 4th my boat was swamped".

By the middle part of the 19th century, large numbers of Chinese had settled in the Northeast, transforming the sleepy riverine communities into busy trading towns. Warehouses and beautiful old colonial houses sprung up along the banks of the river. And in the central markets, silk stalls crowded the alleyways displaying all shades of greens, yellows and reds, as well as animal hides, opium, sugar and ivory horns. Nong Khai and Chiang Khan rapidly developed into thriving entrepots with narrow streets made up of "squalid and untidy houses" clustered along the water front.

From Vientiane, vessels laden with merchandise made their way along the banks shaded with banana and betel palms on their long journey south. Most boats would sail to Paklai from where the cargo was transported to Utaradit by elephant and then down to Bangkok on the Chao Phya River. Alternatively, the cargo could be unloaded at Nong Khai from where it was a nine or ten week journey to Bangkok using carts and pack bullocks.

Even during the early 20th century, the journey was never easy. Marthe Bassenne, a French woman who explored much of French Indochina between 1909-1911, summed up the fears of many travellers in her book 'In Laos and Siam'. "It is possible that we will have to battle against difficulties and face some dangers before making it to our destination," she wrote of her journey through the Lower Mekong and the Northeast of Thailand and Laos "The rapids have rendered many victims; the tiger-infested forest is full of fevers".

Timeless Scenes

Nowadays, beyond the muddy shoreline occasionally fringed with trees laden with jackfruit and papaya, villages and towns have sprung up, collections of corrugated roofs and ugly concrete buildings which mar this tranquil scene. At daybreak, when the gentle heat of the morning has yet to give way to the midday sun, the banks of the river are filled with villagers planting seedlings in the rich soil of the Mekong or carrying water cans in-land to where the plains are dotted with young green shoots. Further from the shores, where the water eddies around rocks and boulders, sand banks are cultivated with neat rows of lettuces, tomatoes and cabbages.

On the river banks, freshly caught fish are left to dry in the sun. Later they will be salted and sold in the markets along with piles of *pla chon* and red snapper still breathing out their last gasp of air.

Against this timeless backdrop, it is easy to be transported back to another age. At dusk shadowy figures of men, women and children still bathe in the river, their laugher ringing out into the dappled evening light. Here on the Mekong, even the arrival of the modern world has failed to find a substitute for a dip in the water, hair matted in shampoo, mouths full of toothpaste. In the shallows too, women clothed only in *sarongs* are hard at work, washing their laundry in the murky pools.

But like the untold moods of this giant river, the scene constantly fluctuates with reminders of the modern world. From a rickety wooden pier nearby, a small fishing boat sets sail powered by a new diesel engine. Further off in the distance, a speed boat glides across the water taking tourists up river, whilst the distant sounds of a karaoke bar occasionally break in on the silence.

River Journey

East of Chiang Khan lies the most beautiful stretch of the river. As the road curves through the hills, sudden rocky outcrops give way to sparsely covered countryside and to distant views of the mighty river meandering past boulders and lofty mountains.

At some points, the road runs parallel to sand banks, at others passing nearby rapids or waterfalls tumbling down the mountainside. But even amidst this natural splendour, stark reminders of the devastation caused by man's greed are never far away. On the southern bank of the river, tracts of forest still cover the mountainside of neighbouring Laos, a profusion of twisted greens and yellows and browns. On Thai soil, the lush trees have gone, victim of short sighted government policies and widespread illegal logging.

Beyond the Kaeng Khut Khu Rapids and the dusty town of Pak Chom, the road passes a few small villages before descending into Sangkhom. From this delightful town, fishermen with drift nets paddle across the misty waters of the Mekong in narrow wooden boats. Occasionally too, villagers come here to scour the banks of the river for gold.

Further east in the town of Nong Khai, the Mekong takes on another guise. In this pleasant provincial town with its spattering of wooden buildings and its famous submerged Laotian Chedi, passenger boats sail too and fro like bobbing corks on the surface of the water. Rising up from the distance, the brand new Friendship Bridge known as *Saphaan Mittaphap* is a more poignant symbol of the future. Built by the Australians and opened in April 1994, it is the first structure to span the Mekong and will eventually link Nong Khai with Vientiane by rail.

Along the river front, hotels and guest houses are slowly replacing the splendid weather-beaten old French colonial architecture with their arched balconies, honey-coloured shutters and rusty door frames. Even the old style markets selling Russian binoculars from communist countries of old are fast disappearing.

Precarious Mood

Yet the mood is as precarious as the waters whipped up into waves by an approaching storm. Beyond Nong Khai, the crowded highways give way to smaller roads and to a landscape dotted with tomato plants and sweet corn. In the trading town of Nakhon Phanom, scene of some of the finest views on the river, hives of fishing boats depart for the Laotian town of Tha Kaek, framed by the hazy outline of the Annamite Mountains.

Along the banks of the river too, is a sight which is prized by Isaan travellers and pilgrims. Shortly before the town of Mukdahan is the holy temple of Wat That Phanom. This Lao style chedi, bedecked with 10 kilograms of gold, is the most famous in the region. In 1975, the shrine collapsed after four days of torrential rains, but was reconstructed under a project funded by the revered King of Thailand, Bhumipol Adulyadej. The daily crowds who descend on it are proof enough of the faith and superstition which are the backbone of this region.

Lifeline

Further south past the towns of Khemmarat and Ban Nam Taeng, the Mae Nam Kong, changes course, weaving its way past small islands, covered in low bamboo scrub and sparse vegetation. Out of the shadows, small fishing boats whip across the surface, their giant engines roaring beneath the weight of twenty five horsepower engines. Occasionally, boat loads of smugglers cross over the water, carrying pigs or gems, silently disappearing over the invisible border.

Nearing the end of its journey through Isaan, the sluggish brown waters of the Mekong, are joined by the clear waters of the River Mun, Thailand's largest tributary and another of the great lifelines of the Northeast. For a brief moment, the water is clouded as the two powerful currents come together. Then the majestic Mekong continues its course, swinging out of Thailand near the town of Kong Chiam and continuing its long journey through Laos and Cambodia before pouring out into the sea through the Mekong Delta in South Vietnam.

Above : Monks at the Kaeng Tana Rapids, Ubon Ratchathani Province.
Right page, top : Journey down the Mekong, Khemmarat, Mukdahan Province. – *bottom* : Cargo Boat, Chiang Khan, Loei Province.
Preceding page : Early morning mists over the Mekong, Sangkhom, Nong Khai Province.
Following pages, left : Rock formations, Kaeng Tana National Park, Ubon Ratchathani Province. – *right* : Downstream, Kantharalek, Si Sa Ket Province.

Above : Unloading cargo, Chiang Khan, Loei Province.
Below : Early morning traffic, Sangkhom, Nong Khai Province.
Left page : Washing in the Heuang River, Loei Province.
Preceding pages : Late afternoon light on the Srindhorn Reservoir, Ubon Ratchathani Province.

77

Misty views over to the Laotian town of Tha Khaek, Nakhon Phanom Province.

Above : Cruising the Mekong, Mukdahan Province.
Following pages : Sunset over the banks of the Mekong, Chiang Khan, Loei Province.

THE HEARTLANDS

In November, the heartlands of Isaan take on a mantle of natural bounty. Endless fields of ripened rice stretch out like a sea of gold, bounded by a distant horizon. Here and there groups of workers labour in the chequered paddies, their metal scythes rising and falling as they edge forward like an army of ants on the move.

In the heartlands of Isaan, the very rhythms of life change in time with the seasons. At harvest time, the working day begins well before dawn when offerings are made to *phi khao* spirit of the rice. Then whole families put aside their domestic tasks to work in the fields. Only when the last golden grains have been picked and taken to the mills does life return to normal, with the new year celebrations marking the end of another cycle on the eternal wheel of nature.

Centuries of rice growing, however, have done little to relieve the hardship of Isaan farmers. Typically most of Thailand has two or three crops a year. But in the Northeast where the soil is arid and sandy, many provinces make do with one crop. Indeed whilst Isaan comprises over 40% of the nation's rice growing area, it produces less than a quarter of the total crop.

Even the monsoon rains can be a mixed blessing. Sometimes they come in torrential outbursts, flooding the surrounding towns and villages. At other times, months go by with barely a fall, sending temperatures up to 40C and leaving the landscape filled with fissures and the dams and fresh water lakes empty.

Generally the first seeds are planted in May and the small squares of paddy irrigated by water from nearby dams or ponds. After four to six weeks, the young green shoots are removed from the seed-bed and transplanted to the neighbouring fields to coincide with the beginning of the monsoon. This is the time when many men from the village will enter the temple with ordinations common place. By the end of October, when the rains have given way to the gentle heat of spring, the heartlands are turned into one vast green mosaic. Then in November, the rice harvest is gathered, the grain chaffed mainly by hand, before being taken to the mills and sold to Chinese merchants.

Curse of Drought

On these sunbaked plains where water buffalo wander impassively against the ochre skies, the curse of drought is never far away. In his award-winning novel 'A Child of the Northeast', Kampoon Boontawee describes how the people of Isaan would often be forced to abandon their homes and journey to other districts where rain was more abundant. For weeks at a time, they would go out in search of fish, frogs and even ants, camping at night under their oxen carts to guard against marauding bands of thieves. Then when the carts were full, they would take the long road home, bartering their new found wealth for rice and for the essentials necessary to take them through another year.

Legends tell how the people of Isaan during really severe droughts chained elephants to wooden posts, hoping that the clashing of their tusks would inspire the gods with fear and bring rain. In more recent times, Siamese cats were placed in cages and carried through the streets whilst the people doused them with water and goaded them with shrill musical instruments. The people believed that the screams of the frightened animals would spur the gods into bringing rain. In some provinces, giant home-made rockets are fired into the clouds, whilst beautifully dressed villagers perform ritual dances to please the celestial beings that inhabit the sky.

Even these time honoured methods however are not enough to ensure plentiful amounts of rain. And whilst government efforts have paved the way for dams throughout the heartlands of Isaan, a bad year will still see farmers walking miles to collect water or watching as their crops slowly wither and turn to dust.

Echoes of the Past

To travel into the heartlands of Isaan is to take a journey back in time and to experience a way of life which in many parts of Thailand has become a faded dream. Here in the small communities, where pigs and chickens are kept beneath the houses, traditions remain an inextricable part of village life and hospitality a gift that is freely handed out to passing strangers.

When the great explorer Henri Mouhot journeyed to the town of Chaiyaphum in February 1861, he required elephants and oxen to traverse the Dong Phya Phai Forest, an area known for its fevers, for its tigers and wretched tracks. On his expedition, he came across an average of only one caravan a day made up of more than 80 teams of oxen. "I am at the gates of the infernal regions, for so the Laotians and Siamese designate this forest, and I have no spell to terrify the demons which inhabit it. If I must die here, where so many other wanderers have left their bones, I shall be ready when my hour comes".

Later travellers found the heartlands to be a mixture of thick forests and plains cleared for the cultivation of rice. "In places we passed through thickly wooded country where enormous leaves at least a foot long were falling from the trees as we passed like autumn at home," wrote Major W.T. Blake, in 1955.

During the mid 1960s, when Isaan was affected by the upheavals in neighbouring Indochina, the Thai government aided by the Americans cleared vast areas of land for cash crops. And now outside of the national parks and wildlife reserves, the lush tropical forests have almost entirely disappeared.

Rice cultivation too has in many places given way to other crops like tapioca, sweet corn, maize and sugar cane which are better suited to the uncertain weather conditions of the Northeast. In Nong Khai Province and along the banks of the Mekong River, you may even catch sight of tomato plants, tobacco plantations and mulberry bushes, sudden bursts of colour on the arid landscape.

Silk Country

As much a part of traditional life in the heartlands as growing rice is the art of silk weaving. This craft is most famous in the provinces of Nakhon Ratchassima, Surin and Khon Kaen, but is also a speciality of countless other small communities dotted throughout the countryside. In some villages, wooden looms and spinning wheels are more common even than bicycles with the beautiful hues of silk, coloured deep blues, reds and orange, displayed in markets and shops around Thailand.

Using an ancient dying process known as *mutmee*, the villagers' first step is to nurture the silk worms on a diet of mulberry leaves until they make their cocoons. When the cocoons are large enough, they are boiled in pots over a wooden fire and the threads carefully extracted by hand. They are then spun on primitive spinning wheels before being tie-dyed and woven into a variety of different patterns. In all the process can take three months from start to finish with the final article costing just a few dollars a meter.

With the support of Queen Sirikit and a variety of foundations, other craft and cottage industries also continue to flourish. In the village of Dan Kwian, near Korat, potters make the traditional glazed water jars that are found outside almost every house. In Renu Nakhon, further to the east, beautiful silk is found along with other brightly coloured fabrics. Elsewhere axe pillows, silverware and even woven baskets are the gifts of Isaan to the world, and the traditions that continue to provide continuity amidst the flux of modern life.

Unexpected Warmth

In the heartlands, there is an unexpected warmth that brings colour to the most barren landscape. It's found in the paddies where groups of children occasionally fish for *pla chon* with long rods of bamboo and wicker baskets. It's found along the dusty tracks leading between the rice fields. Even in the ugly modern towns, a short stroll will take you down narrow alleys lined by ramshackle houses, with narrow canals and the occasional breezy temple.

The markets too are a cacophony of vibrant sounds, smells and colours where the profusion of orchids mingles with the piles of chillis coloured in reds, yellows and greens, and where pigs heads stuck on metal skewers appear to glare disconsolately at passers by. Well before dawn, people are already hard at work cooking giant vats of curry or barbecuing *khai yang* chicken over red hot coals. And late at night, a few vendors remain frying vegetables in large woks, bantering and laughing beneath the flickering lights of the market.

Nearby, in the simple huts and new concrete houses that these people call home, children live with their parents and often their grandparents, sleeping, eating and working side by side. Often when a son marries, he will live in the same compound as his wife's family and will be expected to contribute to the household. As he grows older, his role in the village will take on greater influence. Then his children and his children's children will take up the task where he leaves off, in turn providing support and

respect for the "elders" in the village. Traditionally large families have been viewed as the only way for parents to ensure prosperity in their old age. Despite one of the most successful family planning campaigns in Asia, it is still by no means uncommon to come across families of six or more children.

Nightfall

As night casts a pall over the towns and villages of Isaan, plumes of smoke drift from the burning rice paddies out onto the rolling countryside. Along the narrow roads and dirt tracks that lead to every village, children and old men move slowly across the vast horizon herding cattle. A few water buffalo immerse themselves in pools of water along the roadside, joined occasionally by young boys and girls taking an evening bath. Except for the occasional mini tractor passing by, the scene has changed little in twenty years.

In the villages too, nightfall brings release from the day's labours, as the shouts and screams of children playing ball mingle with the talk of grown ups huddled around small fires preparing food for the evening. Further off, beneath the ubiquitous coloured lights, Isaan singers provide a steady draw to the groups of workers exhausted after the day's toils. Clutching microphones, their shrill voices sing of love and poverty, echoing through the streets and beyond to the houses where children sleep on wooden floors, as many as six or seven to a room.

Traditionally life in the heartlands has continued regardless of events in distant Bangkok. Governments come and go, but so long as rice is abundant, rural life goes on, untrammeled by events beyond. But in Isaan too things are changing. On the outskirts of the major towns, rows of new harvesters and tractors stand as sentinels of the new order. And whilst water buffalo remain the predominant tool of the farmers, even these will soon be little more than a monument to ancient times.

Above : Temple grounds at dawn, Kalasin Province.
Right page, top : Market day, Surin Province. – *bottom* : Commuting in the Northeast, Yasothon Province.
Preceding page : Thrashing the rice in December, Tha Li, Loei Province.

Above : Inside a funeral parlour, Korat, Nakhon Ratchassima Province.
Preceding pages, left : Tricycle driver, Ubon Ratchathani Province. – *righ*t: Herding the water buffalo, Mahasarakham Province.

Old style petrol pump attendant, Udon Thani Province.

Above : Harvesting the rice, Kalasin Province.
Right page, top : Sugar cane farming, Khon Kaen Province. – *bottom* : Sun drying bananas, Sangkhom, Nong Khai Province.
Preceding pages : Early evening in the heartlands, Chaiyaphum Province.

Above : Portrait of village life, Mahasarakham Province.
Right : Street scene, Korat, Nakhon Ratchassima Province.

Above : Milling the rice, Surin Province.

Above : Buffalo and cart, Buriram Province.
Following page : Annual Elephant Round Up, Surin Province.

FESTIVALS OF THE NORTHEAST

At the end of May, as the shimmering heat of the dry season engulfs the plains of the Northeast, the people of Isaan celebrate one of their most timeless and bountiful festivals. In the towns of Yasothon and Roi Et, rockets as tall as houses are fired off into the sky in the belief that they will induce the start of the monsoon rains. Whilst these fantastically decorated missiles hurtle into the air carrying up to 120 kilograms of gunpowder, crowds of drunken revellers dance on wooden stages to the sounds of local rock bands, whilst others submerge themselves in vast pools of mud, entreating the gods of the sky to ensure plentiful rains in the coming season.

According to legend, the festival dates back to the time when the Lord Buddha in one of his many reincarnations was born as a toad. During a period of severe drought, the Lord Buddha called upon Phaya Naki, the giant snake to attack Phaya Dtan, the god of rain, but Phaya Naki was defeated. The Lord Buddha then called upon Phaya Dtaw, the wasp and Phaya Dtan the hornet to attack, but they too were defeated. Finally after platoons of termites, moths and centipedes were sent in to do battle, a pact was agreed. Under the pact, the people promised to send up rockets to remind Phaya Tan to begin the rains. Then when the frogs began to sing and the farmers beat their rattan wind chimes, the monsoons would cease.

These days to make their rockets go higher the villagers first place young virgins astride the missiles, whilst to entertain the spirit of explosives, they play loud Isaan music. *Bungfai* rules dictate that the biggest class of rockets must have no less than 120 kilograms of gun powder, with prizes awarded to the rocket that stays in the sky the longest.

But legends and competition rules provide little more than the backdrop for the people of Isaan to excel in their greatest gift, to party. As giant rockets career off into the sky or skewer dangerously into the nearby paddies, middle aged women covered from head to foot in mud stagger to music played by villagers dressed in pantomime costumes. For two days, nobody sleeps, fueled by whisky, by beer and by sheer euphoria. Then on the Sunday following completion of the inevitable Miss Rocket Beauty Pageant, the people melt away, returning to the surrounding villages, to the rice fields and to the nearby towns, having completed another chapter in the annual cycle.

Joie de Vivre

Throughout the Northeast, festivals are celebrated with a joie de vivre and colour unlike almost anywhere else in Thailand. Some festivals are national occasions which recall the Thai New Year or the end of the rains. Others are purely local events, evidence both of the people's love of song and dance and of the need to escape the rigours and monotony of life in the fields.

The greatest party of all takes place at *Songkran*, which is held in April at the height of the dry season. This national holiday, not only heralds the beginnings of the Thai New Year, but is a time when families get together from all over the country. Early on the first day, the people give food and alms to the monks and sprinkle scented water over images of the Buddha. The water symbolizes purification and ritual cleansing and is a means of gaining merit. It is also largely responsible for the mayhem that follows. For three days, fleets of cars and buses drive around town soaking pedestrians with plastic containers of water. Fire engines with hose pipes join the fray, whilst frantic villagers man the nearby rivers and canals supplying roving bands of water throwers. Even police and politicians are considered fair game in this manifestation of sheer exuberance.

Nor are major festivals the only attraction in Isaan. Often in the small villages, you will come across families celebrating the birth of a daughter or son, or a temple fair where the whole village descends on shooting galleries and big ferris wheels with a relish that even a poor harvest cannot erase.

In the courtyards of Prasat Phimai and Prasat Phanom Rung, annual open-air festivals are held with dazzling light and sound shows and running commentaries of those ancient times. Whilst in the centre of Korat, thousands gather annually to commemorate the most legendary of all figures, Thao Suranari, who in 1826 delivered the town from the Laotian armies of Prince Anuwong.

Elephant Festival

Of all the festivals held in the Northeast, it is the Surin elephant round up that is the most widely known and the most lavishly promoted. Weeks ahead, tourist brochures and local radio stations advertise the charms of the event which is touted as the biggest elephant round up in the world. Truck loads of sugar cane are brought in from far and wide to feed the fleet of giant quadrupeds. Then finally the animals weighing as much as two tons, come lumbering in to town having walked from as far afield as Chaiyaphum and Taklang Village.

The festival's origins are sketchy, but the Thai love of this lumbering animal is well known. In Surin Province, home of the once formidable Suay people, the bond between man and beast is especially strong. Traditionally these mahouts have trained the elephants from birth, working with them in logging camps and in building sites where until recently they were a vital source of

labour. Now that these skills are no longer required, the mahouts have been forced to travel to the big cities in order to make a living. As crowds descend from all over Thailand, some 200 elephants, stomp through the city, sprinting over football pitches and even sparring with their trunks. Wrestling matches, mass battles, even a tug of war are all part of an event which has the mass appeal of a football match, but which demonstrates the immense skills of these once numerous beasts.

At night, it is common to see the mahouts washing their elephants in the river, soaping them down, scrubbing them in the murky water, even talking to them: proof of the special bond that even the touristic displays can never undermine.

Pee Ta Khon

If Surin's claim to fame is its elephants, the tiny village of Dan Sai in the far west corner of Loei Province has a far more bizarre claim to prominence. For most of the year, it is just another small village with one main street and a spattering of craft shops. But for two days in June, it is transformed into one immense gathering of phallic-wielding ghouls and ghosts known as *Pee Ta Khon*.

Nobody knows what the origins of this celebration are, nor the precise significance of the wooden masks and mischievous spirits. But for as long as villagers remember, this two day festival has been a vital part of life in the village and a celebration of fertility and renewal. The event begins with a ceremonial walk by villagers to the medium's house where the *Bai Si* ceremony takes place to the sounds of wailing and chanting. Then, processions of villagers dressed in beautifully carved masks and sporting giant phalluses move down the main street dancing to the sound of bells and the wheezing tunes of a horn.

One legend tells that the procession recalls the time when Prince Vessandorn, the Lord Buddha's penultimate incarnation returned to the city and was welcomed by a procession of spirits.

But even that does not fully explain the parade of locals covered from head to foot in mud, nor the villagers clutching magical pebbles and the bloated white-sheeted male and female monsters dancing down the street. Only in the evening following the inevitable explosion of rockets, does the festival take on a more somber note with the reading of fourteen Buddhist sermons in the local temples, symbol of the reverence that underlies the most joyous festivity.

Religious Festivals

Religion mingles with revelry on other occasions too. During the full moon day that occurs in April or May, almost every man, woman and child in Isaan will attend their local temple to celebrate *Visakha Bucha*, an event which recalls the birth, enlightenment and death of the Buddha. At night in the wats, the faithful circle the temple three times, clutching a candle, flowers and incense. These superstitious people will have their fortune read and make donations in order to gain merit for the next life.

The beginning of the monsoon also heralds other festivities. As the fierce heat of summer dissipates and the dark clouds gather over the plains of Isaan, so the people of the Northeast begin work on giant wax candles. These vast and intricately fashioned beeswax candles depicting stories of the Lord Buddha are paraded through the streets of Ubon Ratchathani and the surrounding towns in July as part of a merit making ceremony. Typically the candles are as big as the trucks which carry them. Processions fill the streets of Ubon with young maidens dressed in blues and greens, accompanied by rain dancers, village bands and floats carrying the village beauty.

The events recall the occasion when the Buddha forbade his followers to travel on a pilgrimage or to stay overnight at any places other than their own temple. The pronouncement was made to save them from trampling mud into people's houses. These days *Khao Phansa*, which is known as the three month rainy retreat, coincides with merit making festivities where the local people offer saffron robes, incense sticks and flowers to the monks. This is also the time when many ordinations take place. During their three months in the temple, the monks will use the light of the candles to study, meditate and teach, exemplifying the traditional values laid down by the Buddha.

End of the Monsoon

By the end of October, the monsoon rains have filled the rivers and lakes of Isaan with water bringing new life and new hope for the people who live on these lands. Where once rocks showed, now the fast flowing current carries the rich soil downstream irrigating the channels and rice paddies. This is the time for harvest and celebration. It is also the time of one of Isaan's best loved festivals.

Along the banks of the River Mun and the River Mekong, giant flotillas of long boats take to the waters manned by teams equipped with wooden paddles. Villagers, whom only months earlier had retreated in doors from the rains, train almost daily in anticipation of the races to come. In Buriram, in Nakhon Phanom and Phimai, fantastically decorated boats decked in red and yellow ribbons, whip through the water at the speed of knots, whilst cheer leaders wave brightly coloured flags and banners from the shore.

The end of the monsoon also heralds other festivals. On the full moon of the 12th lunar month, the locals celebrate *Loi Krathong* by making boats out of banana leaves. On each boat, shaped like a lotus flower, they place a coin and a candle. The locals believe that the *krathong* will carry away their sins and will leave them cleansed for the coming year. In one of the most beautiful ceremonies held in the evening, people of every age launch their *krathongs* out onto ponds, lakes and canals throughout the region, transforming the water into a fairy tale world of lights. It is a fitting way for the people of Isaan to give thanks to the power of water and to celebrate another cycle on the wheel of fortune.

Above & below : Pee Ta Khon masked festival, Dan Sai, Loei Province.
Left page : Procession of gouls, Dan Sai.
Preceding pages : Pee Ta Khon masked festival, Dan Sai, Loei Province.

Above: Village processions, rocket festival, Roi Et Province.
Preceding pages, left : Rocket festival, Yasothon Province.
Right : Boat racing on a tributary of the River Mun, Phimai, Nakhon Ratchassima Province.

Village float, rocket festival, Yasothon Province.

Khao Phansa processions, Ubon Ratchathani Province.

Above and below : Dancers celebrating the July candle festival, Ubon Ratchathani Province.

Songkran water festival, Korat, Nakhon Ratchassima Province.

Traffic jam of water throwers, Songkran festival, Korat.

Above : Annual street parades, Yasothon Province.
Below : Drunken revellers, Yasothon Province.
Right : Village elders, rocket festival, Yasothon Province.

Annual temple fair, Surin Province.

Traditional village 'likay' show, Sakhon Nakhon Province.

Above : Light and sound show, Phimai, Nakhon Ratchassima Province.
Below : Loi Krathong Festival, Korat, Nakhon Ratchassima Province.
Left : Light and sound show, Phimai.
Following pages : Candle festival, Ubon Ratchathani Province.

CHANGING HORIZONS

South of Ban Dhan, the rice fields and tapioca plantations soon give way to factories manufacturing light bulbs, to sprawling warehouses and to new housing developments, harbingers of the modern world in Isaan. Gone are many of the water buffalo, the ox and carts that once trundled down dirt tracks and the street stalls that sold petrol by the bottle. In their place Mitsubishi trucks, spanking new petrol stations and discarded polythene bags that litter both sides of the sealed highway.

In the nearby city of Korat, the contrast is even greater. In this bustling concrete metropolis, a handful of western style fast food shops stand along side karaoke bars, brassy night clubs, hotels and glittering cocktail bars. At one end of town almost hidden behind advertizing plaques and green foliage, lies a sprawling squat, made up of flimsy wooden and corrugated shacks. Yet on the far side of town, a vast area of land is already being cleared for another new housing development which will be sold off to Isaan's emerging middle class.

Little more than 30 years ago, the city of Korat, otherwise known as Nakhon Ratchassima, had a population of less than 20,000 people, mostly small time traders and suppliers. But the advent of the Vietnam war in the late 1960s and early 1970s transformed the town. Overnight, a vast air base was built to accommodate more than 5,000 American soldiers as well as several hundred B52 bombers and other strategic weaponry. Overnight, demand sprang up for waitresses, for bar girls and for staff capable of supporting this international war effort. When the Americans finally withdrew from their bases in the Northeast after the fall of Saigon, other Thais simply moved in to take up the slack.

But if the Americans were the chief purveyors of prosperity in the 1960s and early 1970s, it has been the Thai government that has spurred regional growth in the late 1980s and early 1990s. During the Chatchai administration, unprecedented efforts were made by the government to open up the Northeast and to tap a market with a third of the population and a third of the national vote. Those efforts led to new highways, improved airports, even a free-trade zone in the case of Korat. Not surprisingly, they have also led to a yawning gap between the newly emerging middle class and the traditional rice farmers, who command little support.

Glow of Prosperity

It is a story that is increasingly common throughout the major towns of Isaan. Korat now has a population of more than 250,000, making it the second largest city in Thailand, after Bangkok. Ubon Ratchathani and Khon Kaen both have populations in excess of 200,000. Indeed these new cities are amongst the fastest growing in the whole of the country as agricultural workers pour in from the countryside in search of work.

Further to the north, in the city of Nong Khai, the recently completed Australian sponsored Friendship Bridge across the Mekong River stands as another symbol of the modern world in Isaan. Elsewhere, car show rooms, shopping centres and discotheques with lasers and fabulous sound systems, stand as sentinels of the new order which neither conservationists nor idealists can stem.

Out in the countryside too, the arid plains are already bathed in the first glow of prosperity reflected in the scattering of new motorbikes. Brightly coloured *sarongs*, for decades the fashion around town, have in many cases given way to Levi jeans, American style t-shirts and brightly coloured jackets. Even village fairs occasionally have roundabouts and sometimes bumper cars where the youth get a taste of the big cities that in future will beckon them.

Nowhere is the contrast so striking as in the countryside around Si Sa Ket and Roi Et, where small huts with aerials sprout up from the rice fields like mole hills equipped with space age technology. Some wooden houses now proudly display posters of a local beauty queen on their balconies, others western heart throbs advertizing local soap, toothpaste or other consumer products.

Even in the drought stricken area known as the Weeping Prairies, new farming techniques and the introduction of a variety of different crops have provided at least some respite. Soil that was barely able to support one rice crop now supports green rows of vegetables, carrots, tomatoes and tapioca. New dams and irrigation channels have also sprung up in many areas, the result of concerted efforts by the country's beloved King Bhumipol and his advisors.

Further Education

The influx of money has already brought unheard of wealth to some landowners and traders. Many self-made businessmen and women now sport brand new cars and occasionally even portable telephones. The first thing that most families aspire to is a motorbike and a blaring radio.

Like the new dams which are scattered over the plains of Isaan and the re-afforestation programs which promise to reverse the rape of its forests, progress is also bringing hope to people who once had only poverty to look forward to. Children whose destiny it was to work the fields, now learn to read and write in schools. Whereas the vast majority would leave school at the age of fourteen, now greater numbers are staying on for further education encouraged by the idea of a full time career or simply the prospects of taking a job outside of the countryside. These days, there is even a technological university in Korat, turning out engineers and the other vital human resources which are so desperately needed if Isaan is to shape itself a brighter future.

Mixed Blessing

But like a two edged sword, the rapid pace of change is causing problems for many Isaan people. In the past every man, woman and child took to the fields to plant or harvest the rice crop. Now many farmers find it faster and cheaper to rent a tractor. Greater use of machinery has led to higher efficiency and increased profits for the big landowners. It has also reduced the need for seasonal workers who traditionally relied on labour in the rice fields to supplement their meagre earnings elsewhere. Unemployment, until recently unknown, has in some districts reached alarming levels, exacerbating the growing gap between rich and poor. And that crisis in turn has led to a dramatic increase in migration as the people of Isaan are forced to leave their homes and families in search of work.

Around Korat and Ubon Ratchathani, especially, salt farms and re-afforestation schemes have caused environmental degradation, striking discord in once unified communities. So too the vast river dams which generate much needed electricity for the country at large, but which often provide few benefits for the local people who rely on the land for survival.

Every year, more than one million seasonal migrants flood the streets of Bangkok and the other major cities, prompted by the need for a job or simply the hope of freedom and wealth. Many of those who come to seek their fortune will find work as taxi drivers, construction workers or hawkers. Others turn to prostitution as a way to lift themselves and their families above the level of poverty. In Bangkok especially, whole communities have sprung up in the sprawling districts of Klongtoey and Din Daeng catering to the daily influx of workers who arrive by train and by bus to start their new lives. The majority of workers view their stay in the cities as temporary. But few of those who depart Isaan will return to their native lands to take up the plough and uphold the traditions that have supported so many earlier generations.

Borderlines

The seeds of change are more than anywhere being sewn along the border with Cambodia and Laos where the battle fields of Indochina are rapidly giving way to a market place. At Mukdahan and Nakhon Phanom, towns which until recently most Thais had never heard of, hotels and shopping centres are springing up alongside the traditional street markets. Border trade between these bustling provincial capitals and the Laotian towns of Savannakhet and Tha Khaek across the Mekong River, is now estimated to run into millions of dollars every week. And volumes continue to grow.

Every day convoys of trucks cross over the Mekong River at Nong Khai piled high with toothpaste, milk powder and other western goods bound for Vientiane, for Laem Prabang and beyond. In future these same convoys may also cross over to Laos from the town of Mukdahan, slated to be home of the next bridge over the Mekong.

Dreams that Isaan may one day become the gateway to Indochina have spurred even more ambitious plans for development. Over the next twenty years, the government aims to transform the region into a major transport hub with a network of roads and bridges connecting up with Vietnam and even China. Tourism too could offer a brighter future as visitors turn away from the crowded beaches and well known sites elsewhere in Thailand to concentrate on an area where cultural and rural life and traditions remain intact.

Uncertain Future

But whilst new roads, new bridges and new ideas will inevitably lead to increased prosperity, they also threaten to unleash even greater changes on the forgotten provinces of Isaan, eroding the values that have given the people their dignity and their spiritual integrity. Already the code which bound the people of Isaan together, a code handed down from parents and grandparents has begun to fray at the edges as social pressures take their toll. Geographical, language and cultural barriers also mean that the people of Isaan are unlikely to reap the opportunities that are available to their richer and better educated neighbours in the Central Plains.

When Pira Sudham wrote of Isaan in the 1980s, he talked of the socio-economic and political changes transforming the rural communities. Nobody who witnesses the momentous changes can fail to share the excitement of the people as they confront the modern world. But how will these same people survive in an environment without the traditional family and religious values that for generations have nurtured them ?

Arriving in Korat, on the last leg of my journey I wandered into the new shopping centers and the car show rooms, into the slums where those in search of the new dreams have ended up, and I wondered if progress can really bring the people of Isaan values enough to make up for the traditions that they are fast losing.

And so it was, one March morning, that I simply packed my bags and left, back down the road that threaded through the plains of Isaan, back to Bangkok and the polluted modern world.

New year's eve party, Chaiyaphum Province.

Nightclubbing in Chaiyaphum Province.

Housing estate, Khon Kaen Province.

Street scene, Chiang Khan, Loei Province.

Above and below : Textile factory, Loei Province.
Left : Village barber's shop, Tha Li District, Loei Province.
Following pages, left : Monsoon season, Buriram Province. – *Right* : Striking modern architecture at
Wat Sala Loi, Nakhon Ratchassima Province.

Railway terminus, Korat, Nakhon Ratchassima Province.

Raising the flag ceremony, Surin Province.

Above : New shopping centre, Udon Thani Province.
Below : Train passengers, Si Sa Ket Province.
*Righ*t : Misty mornings, Ban Pak Huay, Loei Province. *Following pages* : Night market, Surin Province.
– and : Sunrise on the Mekong, Sangkhom, Nong Khai Province.